Mouse Count

P9-CAD-133

Ellen Stoll Walsh

A Voyager Book

Harcourt Brace & Company

SAN DIEGO   NEW YORK   LONDON

Copyright © 1991 by Ellen Stoll Walsh

All rights reserved. No part of this publication may be reproduced or transmitted in any form or by any means, electronic or mechanical, including photocopy, recording, or any information storage and retrieval system, without permission in writing from the publisher.

Requests for permission to make copies of any part of the work should be mailed to: Permissions Department, Harcourt Brace & Company, 6277 Sea Harbor Drive, Orlando, Florida 32887-6777.

Library of Congress Cataloging-in-Publication Data
Walsh, Ellen Stoll.
Mouse count/Ellen Stoll Walsh.
p.   cm.
Summary: Ten mice outsmart a hungry snake.
ISBN 0-15-201050-5
[1. Mice—Fiction. 2. Snakes—Fiction. 3. Counting.] I. Title.
PZ7.W1675Mn   1991
[E]—dc20   90-35915

Special Edition for Trumpet Book Fairs

A B C D E

Printed in Singapore

The illustrations in this book are cut-paper collage.
The text type was set in ITC Modern by the Photocomposition Center, Harcourt Brace & Company, San Diego, California.
Printed and bound by Tien Wah Press, Singapore
This book was printed with soya-based inks on Leykam recycled paper, which contains more than 20 percent postconsumer waste and has a total recycled content of at least 50 percent.
Production supervision by Warren Wallerstein and Ginger Boyer
Designed by Nancy J. Ponichtera and Camilla Filancia

For my nine sisters and brothers:
Sally, Leila, Mary, Nancy, Jane, Betsy,
Joe, George, and John,

and especially for Sally, the eldest,
and her husband, Jay,
intrepid seekers after truth.

GATE GATE PARAGATE PARASAMGATE
BODHI SWAHA!

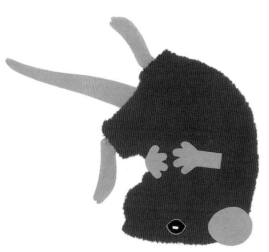

One fine day, some mice played in the meadow.
They were careful to watch for snakes.

But when the mice got sleepy, they forgot about snakes . . .

and they all took naps.

While they slept, a hungry snake went looking for dinner. On his way he found a nice big jar.

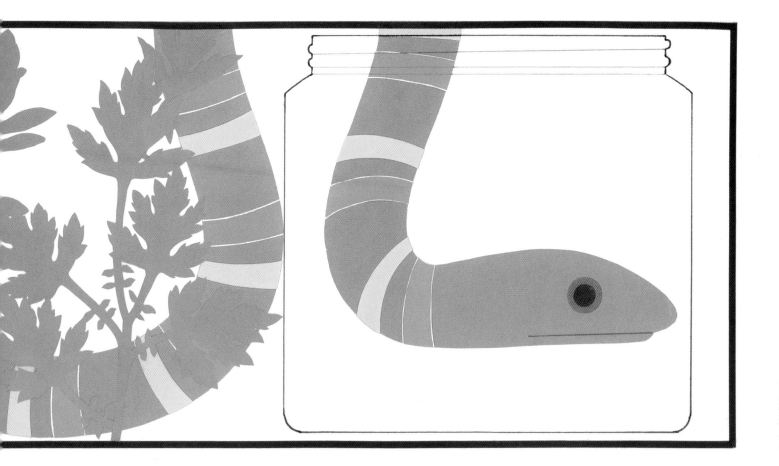

"I will fill this jar with dinner," he said.

It wasn't long before he found three mice—little, warm, and tasty, fast asleep.

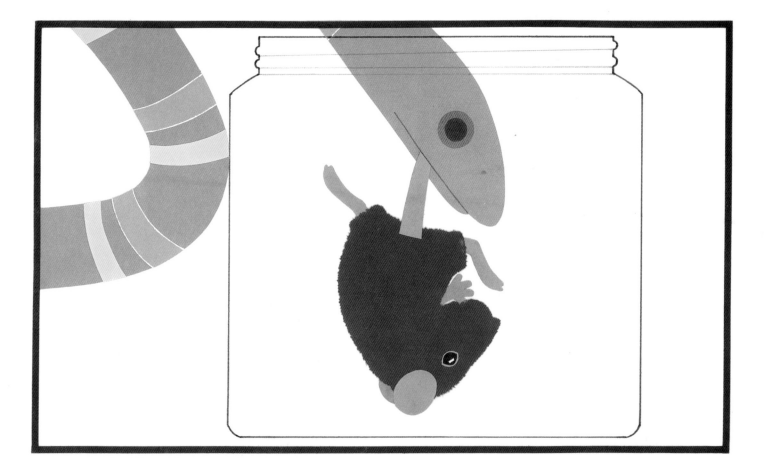

"First I will count them and then I will eat them up," said the snake. "Mouse Count! One . . .

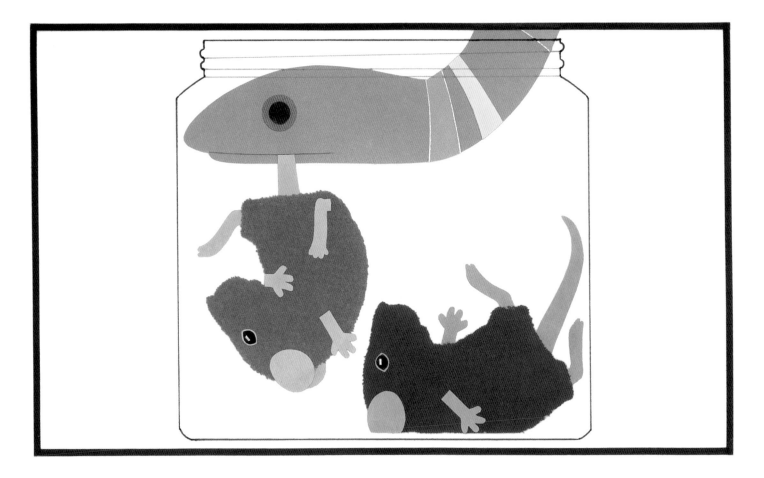

two . . .

three." He dropped them into the jar. But he was very hungry. Three mice were not enough.

Soon he found four more mice—little, warm, and tasty, fast asleep.

And he counted them: "Four . . .

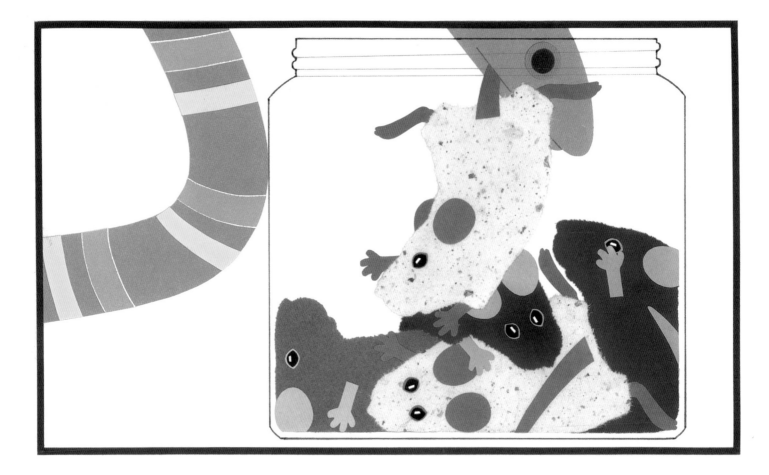

five . . .

six . . .

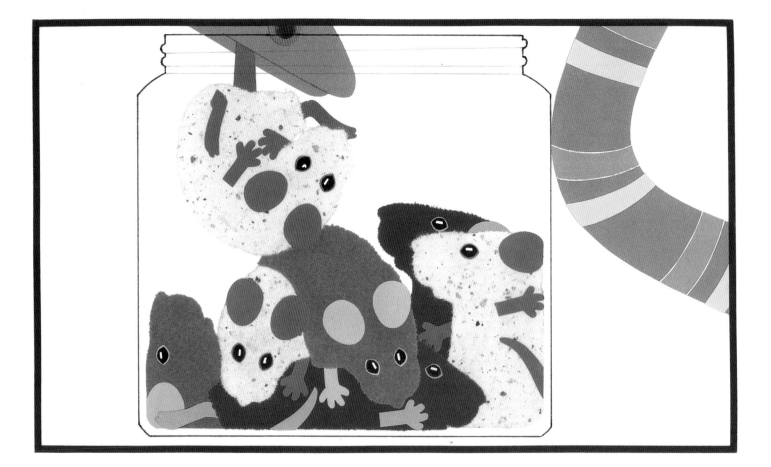

seven." But the snake was very, very hungry,
and seven mice were not enough.

At last he found three more mice—little, warm, and tasty, fast asleep. And he counted them:

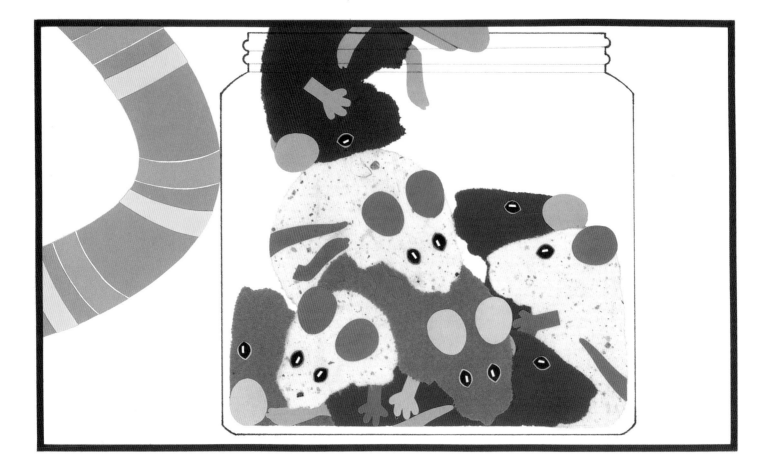

"Eight . . .

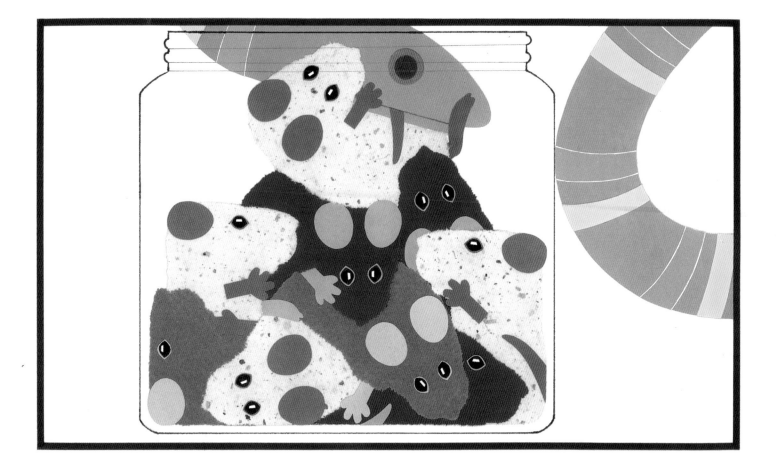

nine . . .

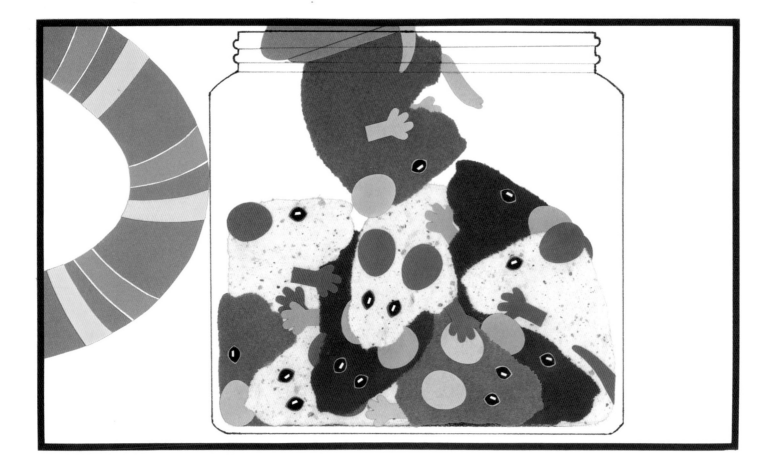

ten."

"Ten mice are enough. Now I am going to eat
you up, little, warm, and tasty," said the snake.

"Wait," said one of the mice. "The jar isn't full yet. And look at the big mouse over there."

The snake was very greedy. He hurried off to get the big mouse.

And while he was gone, the mice rocked the jar one way,

and another way,

until over it went.
"Ten, nine, eight, seven, six, five, four,

three, two, one." The little mice uncounted
themselves and ran home.

The snake reached the big mouse, but it was only
a cold, hard rock.

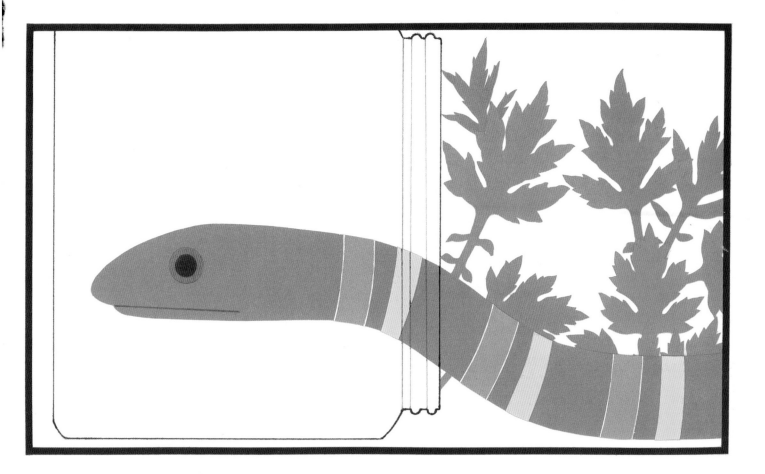

And when he got back, the jar was empty.